THE AMERICAN LANDSCAPE

GREAT PLAINS

DWAYNE HICKS

PowerKiDS press

Published in 2026 by The Rosen Publishing Group, Inc.
2544 Clinton Street, Buffalo, NY 14224

First Edition

Editor: Greg Roza
Book Design: Michael Flynn

Photo Credits: Cover, p. 1 Michael Gordon/Shutterstock.com; (series background) Omeris/Shutterstock.com; p. 5 KensCanning/Shutterstock.com; p. 7 zelvan/Shutterstock.com; p. 9 Menno van der Haven/Shutterstock.com; p. 11 (bison) Jim_Brown_Photography/Shutterstock.com; p. 11 (prairie dog) vadimserebrenikov/Shutterstock.com; p. 13 johannas-pics/Shutterstock.com; pp. 15, 17, 19 Everett Collection/Shutterstock.com; p. 21 tony Franzwa/Shutterstock.com.

Library of Congress Cataloging-in-Publication Data

Names: Hicks, Dwayne, author.
Title: Great Plains / Dwayne Hicks.
Description: Buffalo : PowerKids Press, [2025] | Series: The American landscape | Includes index.
Identifiers: LCCN 2024044862 (print) | LCCN 2024044863 (ebook) | ISBN 9781499450989 (library binding) | ISBN 9781499450972 (paperback) | ISBN 9781499450996 (ebook)
Subjects: LCSH: Great Plains–Juvenile literature.
Classification: LCC F591 .H55 2025 (print) | LCC F591 (ebook) | DDC 978–dc23/eng/20241031
LC record available at https://lccn.loc.gov/2024044862
LC ebook record available at https://lccn.loc.gov/2024044863

Manufactured in China

CPSIA Compliance Information: Batch #QSPK26. For Further Information contact Rosen Publishing at 1-800-237-9932.

CONTENTS

Flat Land

A plain is a large area—or piece of land—that's mostly flat with few trees. Plains are also known as prairies and grasslands. The Great Plains of North America is one of the largest plains in the world! It's home to many kinds of animals, plants, and people!

Where Is It?

The Great Plains is in the middle of the United States. It reaches from central Texas to southern Canada. To the west are the Rocky Mountains. The Mississippi River is east of the Great Plains. Denver, Colorado, is the largest U.S. city in the Great Plains.

ROCKY MOUNTAINS
CANADA
GREAT PLAINS
MISSISSIPPI RIVER
Denver
COLORADO
MEXICO

What's the Weather?

Since the Great Plains are so big, the weather can be very different in different places. In the north, winters are cold and snowy. In the south, summers are hot and sunny. A large part of the Great Plains often has **tornadoes**. In fact, this area is often called Tornado Alley!

Plains Mammals

Many animals live in the Great Plains, but a few are well known. Prairie dogs are small **mammals** that live all over the Great Plains. Bison are large mammals that walk the plains and **graze** on its grasses. Other plains mammals are raccoons, porcupines, elk, bears, and more.

prairie dog
bison

Plains Plants

Many types of plants grow in the Great Plains. Some of the most common plants are grasses. Among them are buffalo grass, needlegrass, wheat, and more. The Great Plains is also home to many types of wildflowers. Sunflowers are one of the most common wildflowers on the Great Plains.

Native Americans

For thousands of years, the Great Plains has been home to many Native American groups. They grew many **crops**, such as maize (corn). They hunted plains animals for food. To do this, they often moved from place to place. They carried their homes with them!

Settling on the Plains

The United States became a country in the late 1700s. Soon after, European Americans began settling on the Great Plains. Many people farmed the land. Some people started **ranches**. In time, many communities grew into centers of business. Today, some of these early farm communities are big cities!

The Dust Bowl

Farming remained very important to Great Plains communities well into the 1900s. Bad farming practices led to problems in the southern plains. The soil dried up and blew away! The soil covered homes and roads. Few farmers could grow crops. This area became known as the Dust Bowl.

Modern Farming

Thanks to better farming practices, the Great Plains is perfect for farming once again. New **technology** helps grow food. Common plains crops are corn, wheat, and soy. This food feeds people all over the United States! Ranches raise all kinds of livestock, such as cows, sheep, and horses.

GLOSSARY

crop: A plant grown on a farm.

graze: To feed on naturally growing grasses.

mammal: Any warm-blooded animal whose babies drink milk and whose body is covered with hair or fur.

ranch: A farm where livestock is raised.

technology: A method that uses science to solve problems and the tools used to solve those problems.

tornado: A strong spinning wind that forms a funnel-shaped cloud that moves in a narrow path over the land.

FOR MORE INFORMATION

BOOKS

Becker, Trudy. *The Dust Bowl*. Mendota Heights, MN: Apex Editions, 2024.

Jaycox, Jaclyn. *Tornadoes*. North Mankato, MN: Pebble, 2022.

WEBSITES

Kiddle: Great Plains Facts for Kids
kids.kiddle.co/Great_Plains
Learn more about the Great Plains at this informative website.

Native People of the American Great Plains
kids.nationalgeographic.com/history/article/native-people-of-the-american-great-plains
Read more about the people and cultures of the Native Americans of the Great Plains.

INDEX